7 Sketches for 7 Songs

DRAMA AND MUSIC PAIRINGS FOR WORSHIP

COMPILED BY KIMBERLY R. MESSER AND GEORGE BALDWIN

Lillenas PUBLISHING COMPANY

KANSAS CITY, MO 64141

Questions? Please write or call:
    Lillenas Publishing Company
    Drama Resources
    P.O. Box 419527
    Kansas City, MO 64141
    Phone: 816-931-1900 ● Fax: 816-412-8390
    E-mail: drama@lillenas.com
    Web site: www.lillenasdrama.com

Cover art by Keith Alexander

Contents

General Notes

Various notes have been provided with each script for setting, props, costumes, and production. Following each piece you'll also find Director's and Actor's Tips that were written after these sketches were staged in front of an audience.

Near the end of each script, look for an asterisk. If you are performing a script with the suggested choral anthem, use this point as cue point to start the music. If you are using the accompaniment track, be sure to have the sound technician to fade the track in at an appropriate volume level under the last lines of dialogue. Whether using a live choir or track, practice this transition several times with the choir and musicians or sound technician to make it as smooth as possible.

Starting Over Again

To be performed with the choral octavo
I Need You More with *I Need Thee Every Hour*

Use: General

Scripture Reference: "Therefore, if anyone is in Christ, he is a new creation; the old has gone, the new has come!" (2 Corinthians 5:17).

Theme: The mercy of God in forgiving us and giving us hope and another chance

Cast: MAN or WOMAN—dejected at first, becoming more hopeful toward the end

Props: Character could use a long fireplace match and a candle with tall sides, burned down inside

Running Time: 3 minutes

> A new start
> Another new start
> Again, I start over again
>
> It's hard to hope, Father!
> It's hard to dream
> It's hard to believe
> That I can change
>
> Help Thou mine unbelief!
>
> Only You can rekindle that spark—
> I can't find a match long enough
> To reach down in there and ignite
> My jaded, disillusioned candle .
>
> I don't believe in me anymore, Lord.
> I can't make me succeed
> I can't win
> And losing hurts
> And losing repeatedly hurts repeatedly

"Starting Over Again" is taken from FIRST PERSON SINGULAR © 1995 by Judith I. Keefe.

Will You help?
Will You put Your Spirit in me
To live through me?
Will You spark that unreachable place?
Will You incline my heart to You,
To obedience
To growth
To maturity?
I do believe in YOU still—
I do believe You live in me—
And I do offer You
This failure-of-a-person
The going-down-for-the-count-again creature

Only You
Living through me
Can win this one, Lord

*If You will help,
I will trust
In You—
Not in me

And just maybe
We
Will win
This time

*Start music here

Director's Tips: Not much space or movement used, so every movement (body or stage-wise) is extremely important. Look up only when necessary, stand at a key point such as noted in "Actor's Tips." Sincerity is key in line delivery.

Actor's Tips: The most important thing to do in making your performance powerful is to have a definite point of change when the character goes from feeling defeated to feeling God's mercy bring hope. Both emotions need to be deeply felt by the actor.

There is not a lot of physical action written into the script so begin by sitting on the ground to indicate how low the character feels at the beginning. As the character begins pleading with God, at the line "Will You help?" move to your knees. As the character begins to feel hopeful about what God can do in his or her life, in the line "I do believe in YOU still," stand to indicate how God lifts him or her up and gives hope to him or her again. This provides various levels to make the piece more visually interesting.

Tips by Chad & Stacey Schnarr.

I Need You More with *I Need Thee Every Hour,* words & music by Lindell Cooley & Bruce Hayes; arranged by Marty Parks

Listening Cassette TA-610C
Listening CD DC-601
Orchestration, Score and Parts OR-2515
Stereo & Split-Trax Accomp CD (both formats included) MU-5533T
Acc Cass w/Demo MU-2515D
"Starting Over Again," **FIRST PERSON SINGULAR** (MP-761), by Judith I. Keefe.

Joyous Troubles

To be performed with the choral octavo *You Are God*

Use: General

Scripture Reference: "Consider it pure joy, my brothers, whenever you face trials of many kinds" (James 1:2).

Theme: Was God serious when He told us to take joy in our trials?

Cast: MAN or WOMAN

Setting: No specific setting is needed

Props: Pink slip
Pocket Bible

Production Notes: This piece was originally performed before a sermon on James 1:2.

Running Time: 4 minutes

(The MAN *or* WOMAN *enters, throwing a pink slip on the ground, stomping it, kicking it, mumbling at it.)*

Layoffs! Shmayoffs! Payoffs! Shoobehemenayoffs! Laid off! I needed that job! I *needed* that job. Oh, I'm weak. How am I gonna live? How am I gonna feed my family? How am I going to pay my bills? Ohhhhh! the *bills!*

(Sitting down in a clump. Pause. Speaks to God.)

God, this is not a good day. No, this is what I would call a bad day, a none so good day, nada good in this day. Now, I'm not saying it's Your fault. I'm saying . . . well . . . it just seems like You could have helped me out a little. Why didn't You axe Kasten? He's an atheist! When push comes to shove, aren't You supposed to go to bat for me?

I'm sorry. I'm just blown away here. I need some help. *(As if responding to God)* You're right. I'll go to the good book, Your pages of peace—the Bible. Where to look . . . How about the Book of James? Yeah, I think so— James, practical James. *(Reading from James 1:2, NIV)* "Consider it pure joy, my brothers, whenever you face trials of many kinds." *(A slow look of contempt up to God.)* I'm gonna read that again. "Consider it pure joy, my

---

brothers, whenever you face trials of many kinds." *(Another look to God)* You've got to be kidding me. So . . . what . . . You want me to say, "Hallelujah! I just got laid off!" Is that what You want? How about, "Praise the Lord! I just went bankrupt!" Or "Whoopee! They're gonna repossess my car!" God, this is not going to be easy. I mean, think about it. I'm gonna walk home, open the door, look at the family, and say, "Rejoice, all, we're going to starve!" And then . . . what . . . do You think the kids are going to follow my lead and jump up and down and say, "That's OK, Daddy [or Mommy], we didn't want any Christmas presents this year anyway." And my wife [or husband] . . . what . . . do you think she's [he's] going to dance a little jig on the couch when she hears these joy-filled tidings? Maybe after dinner the whole merry clan of us can dance over to Grandma's house to hear my ever-so-understanding mother-in-law [father-in-law] say, "Boy, you all look cheery. What's up?" And I'll say, "Dear Grandma, haven't you heard the news? I just got laid off!" And Grandma will say, "Boy, you all seem to be handling it OK." And I'll say, "OK? Grandma, we consider it pure joy!"

You know what, God, I think this verse proves You have a sense of humor. That's what I think. *(Walks off mumbling)* Pure joy! Ha! "Hey, friend, I just totaled my car. Hallelujah!" "Hey, Mom, I just ran over your cat. Amen!" *Pure joy? I don't know . . . *(Exits)*

Start music here

Director's Tips: Allow for the actor to use a fair amount of room. Use all areas of the stage, some to suggest different places.

Actor's Tips: You really have to sell-out and lose all inhibitions for this monologue. It won't play if you casually complain throughout the piece.

Tips by Chris Todd

You Are God (AG-1099), words & music by Sam, Jesse, Joe, John, and James Katina, arranged by Richard Kingsmore
   Octavo Demo Cassette   TA-607C
   Octavo Demo CD   DC-607
   Orchestration, Score and Parts   OR-2490
   Stereo & Split-Trax Accomp CD (both formats included)   MU-5049T
   Acc Cass w/Demo   MU-2490D
"Joyous Troubles," **WORSHIP DRAMA LIBRARY, VOL. 12** (MP-712), by Brad Kindall.

Other Performance Option:

Perform this piece with *There Is Joy in the Lord* (AG-1086). Visit lillenas.com for sound samples.

Putting It Together

To be performed with the choral octavo
A Cradle in the Shadow of the Cross

Use: Christmas

Cast: JOSEPH—a young man in his 20s

Props: Milk bucket
> Tool box (sand paper, hammer, nails, knife)
> Coleman lantern
> Half barrel
> Cradle legs

Setting: Outside a stable in Bethlehem on Christmas morning

Costume Notes: Modern dress

Production Notes:

How many of us are depressed that we can't give the gifts we really want to give on Christmas? Either time or money prevent us. In "Putting It Together," Joseph echoes these same feelings. If only he'd had enough money, Mary wouldn't be having a baby in a stable.

But Joseph doesn't have his eyes on the full picture of what Christmas is all about. God is in control. What we have to offer is nothing compared with what He has to give—as the final moments of the play express for us.

Running Time: 8-10 minutes

(It is near dawn. Crickets. JOSEPH is sitting on an overturned milk bucket. Hay is strewn around at his feet. He is dressed in torn jeans, boots, work shirt, heavy coat, and cap. A tool box sits open at his feet. He is sanding a halved barrel or crate, smoothing off the rough spots. As he speaks, he will also whittle and fit two curved supports, creating a makeshift cradle. A Coleman lantern burns nearby.)

Money. That's the bottom line of it all, isn't it? The fact is, if I had money, do you think she'd be in a place like this tonight? I don't think so. She . . . she'd be lying in some warm sheets somewhere and I'd be dozing off in some overstuffed chair watching her and the baby sleep. I could have had people around her while she was in pain. They could've told her everything would be fine. That everything was normal. That she was do-

---

"Putting It Together" by Lawrence G. Enscoe is taken from WRAPPINGS © 1989 by Lillenas Publishing Company.

ing just great. Instead she had me. All thumbs, unless there's a hammer in my hand. I'm starin' down at her telling her everything is going just right, and all the while my heart's beating so hard, I can't believe it didn't shake loose and fall into my stomach. *(Breaks)* I mean, He's coming into the world, and I didn't even have time to wash my hands.

(Pause. Takes a deep breath.)

Money. That's what it'd take. But what've I got? An honest job that can't even make her comfortable at a time like this. I've never been able to give her what I want to. I married her and I was broke. I worked my fingers raw. I broke my back to prepare for the baby and then somethin' like this comes along and takes everything. There's always some expense you didn't figure on to knock you right back where you started. Travel expenses to Bethlehem. Who would've counted on it?

(Pause.)

I'm so humiliated. I wanted to buy nice things for her. New clothes for the baby. Forget all that. I thought at least I could get her a clean room to have the baby in. You can bet if I'd've thrown some green in that manager's face, he would've let us in. He'd've found something for us. But he took one look at these callouses, these sides of beef for hands with the black, cracked nails, and he knew what he'd get out of the deal. There goes the door. Right in my face. His fat wife probably slept under a feather quilt tonight.

(Pause. He begins to cry.)

Mary. I'm so sorry. I did my best. I don't know why all this happened. Dear God, what does all this mean? Angels whispered in my dreams. They told me not to be afraid. But tonight, I'm terrified. I sat in there while she cried and screamed and I was very afraid. How could You let this happen? Are You testing us? What are You trying to do?

(Begins working harder on the cradle.)

Well, I'll tell You what I'm going to do. I'm getting Him out of that filthy manger, that's what. I'm sure those shepherds You told didn't mind seeing Him like that, but I don't think a king's life should be started in a food trough. He was promised a throne. The least I can do is make Him a cradle. It's something I know I can do, anyway.

(Looks off.)

Look at all those people whooping it up in that inn. Place is packed to the walls, and none've 'em know what's going on right outside their doorstep. Why didn't You tell any of them in there? Who do You tell the wonderful news? Shepherds. They come trundling in babbling about angels and offering us goat cheese sandwiches. Look, I'm not saying they're not good men. I'm not saying anything against them. It's just, who's going to listen to 'em? The story of the birth of the Son of God is going to die out around a campfire out in the fields somewhere. No one's ever going to know. Hah! Maybe that's good. What would people think if they found out anyway? They'd laugh at Him is what they'd do. They'll wonder why I couldn't have done any better for Him.

(Begins fitting the legs on the cradle.)

I don't know what You've got planned for Him with a beginning like this. What's on Your mind? Will they listen to Him? Will they give Him a better reception than this?

(Pulls out a nail and sets it against the cradle leg.)

*If people couldn't find room for a baby in the middle of the night, what'll they do when they find out He's the Son of God?

Start music here

(He begins hammering nail into wood. We listen to the pounding as the lights go to blackout.)

Director's Tips: We didn't follow the exact stage business the script called for. Some type of business, while sitting, is mandatory. Does not need a lot of space, but don't use the power areas of the stage too quickly.

Actor's Tips: Present this in an easy-going, very conversational style. The key is to establish Joseph as VERY likeable. The more the audience sides/connects with him, the better the piece's impact. Definitely pick your spots of reference for this piece.

Tips by Chad Schnarr & Chris Todd.

A Cradle in the Shadow of the Cross (AN-3927), words & music by Dorothy L. Smith, arranged by Richard Kingsmore
   Orchestration, Score and Parts   OR-2455
   Stereo & Split-Trax Accomp CD (both formats included)   MU-5519T
   Acc Cass w/Demo   MU-2455
"Putting It Together," **WRAPPINGS** (MC-271), by Lawrence G. Enscoe.

The Word Is Given

To be performed with the choral octavo *O Come, All Ye Faithful*

Use: Christmas

Cast: G. B.—played by a man or a woman

Setting: A waiting room or lobby on Christmas Eve

Props: Metal chairs
  White jacket (with "The Messengers" written on the back)
  Battered horn case
  Potted plant
  Small table
  Lamp
  Low coffee table
  Magazines
  Table-sized Christmas tree
  2 free-standing door frames

Costume Notes:

Modern costume. One can play with the angel idea in costuming the monologue, however. White shirt. White sweat shirt with musical notes on it. Even a white tux. Wing-tipped shoes?

Production Notes:

A horn player waiting to hear the word that his Christmas concert is on. A tuneless world waiting to hear the sweetest music of all time. This is a perfect match. Especially when the horn player is an angel. Gabriel, no less.

I've always wondered how the angels felt, watching all the Christmas Eve events transpire, and waiting for the moment when they could play their part in the Bethlehem story. This play is a product of that wonderment.

Don't tip your hand that G. B. is Gabriel too early. Play with the modern extended metaphor, allowing the audience to begin making the connections for themselves.

Running Time: 10-12 minutes

(*A waiting room. Several uncomfortable metal-and-vinyl chairs. A white jacket is thrown over the back of one of the chairs and a battered horn case sits on one of the seats. A potted plant, a table with a lamp, a low table with outdated magazines, and a table-sized Christmas tree with tinsel are on the set. A free-standing door frame stands UP LEFT [leading into an office]. Another stands DOWN RIGHT [leading outside]. At lights, G. B. is sitting in a chair and thumbing through a magazine, anxiously. G. B. sighs and looks up, touches the tree, sighs again, and looks up at door U.L., putting magazine down.)*

(G. B., *standing*): He said just a few more minutes. What's taking Him so long? It's been ages. *(Sighs, then laughs.)* I keep forgetting. His sense of time and mine are two very different things.

(Goes to case and starts to open it. Thinks again and, goes to door U.L. and looks inside. Smiles.)

Hi.

(Sighs and walks to door D.R. and looks out.)

So it's finally the Big Night. I've been looking forward to this for a long time. *(Stares)* Look at all of 'em out there, pushing and shoving. Not a pretty sight. It's been crazy like this all day. People have been running their heads off. Packing themselves into the city. Filling up all the shops, the restaurants. I don't think anyone's said a civil word to one another all day. And now that it's night, nothing's gotten any better. Colder than the North Pole out there, and some folks still haven't got a place to sleep. It's not right. *(Pause)* Peace on earth looks a long way off from where I'm standing. And if something like tonight can't turn things around, I don't know what will. *(Pause)* Strange. What people have got right under their noses and they don't even know it. At least they don't act like they know it.

(Pause)

I wonder if there's time for second thoughts?

(Paces. Picks up the horn case.)

Come on. I'm ready. I've been waiting in here forever. I don't know what He's doing in there. What's the delay? I need to get out there. I've got to get to work. This gig is really important tonight. Probably the most important one I'll ever play.

(Goes to door U.L.)

Is He . . . ? No, I know He'll tell me when He's ready. I'm just antsy about it, that's all. The wait feels like it's killing me. You have any idea how—? I know. *(Laughs)* Well, He knows where to find me.

(Paces)

I shouldn't be complaining, I suppose. *(Jerking a thumb at the door U.L.)* He likes to take His time with people. Patient. He cares about them as individuals is the point. That's why I stay with Him. People just don't know how fortunate they are to have someone like Him love them so much.

(G. B. goes to the door D.R.)

Yeah. Tonight's the Big Night. Oh, and it's a beautiful one, too. All the stars are out. That makes it just right, I think. Look at that star over there! That's perfect. This whole night is going to turn out perfect. I can feel it already. What a holiday we're going to have! Everything is on track so far. Except for this hurry-up-and-wait routine. You don't think He's forgotten about me in there?

(Strides to the door U.L.)

Sorry to bother You again, but I don't know how much longer I can wait. The suspense is getting to me out here. No, I'm not trying to rush anyone. I'm just . . . excited. Well, You know what night this is. Everybody's excited around here. Everybody just can't wait to get out there. *(Smiles)* OK. Sure, I understand. Just give me the high sign, will You?

(Paces. G. B. opens horn case, takes out some notes. Begins mouthing the words, quietly, as if memorizing something. Nods and puts paper away.)

What I have to do won't take long. I just need to get out there and do it. *(Pause. Sits. Looks at the tree for a moment.)* It's really something to think about, though, isn't it? The whole thing. Not the crowds, the smells in the air, the jam-packed businesses. I'm talking about the heart of the whole thing. I'm talking about a poor carpenter. His poor young wife. Trudging all those miles on a donkey. And then tonight, there's no place but a stable. A poor woman has a shivering baby in a filthy manger. Animals are the only witnesses to what should be the greatest birth in history. And they're only watching because they're waiting to see if they're going to get their bedroom back.

(Pause)

The whole thing turned out so different than I first thought. *(Looks out)* What did I expect? A warm reception? They're not exactly known for rolling out the red carpet out there.

(Pause)

Still, I'm wondering if this whole thing isn't just a bit too . . . subtle, though. I'm just wondering if people, in all the bustle today, if anyone'll catch a sense of the bittersweet melody of the whole scene. I mean, a baby born in a stable in a one-horse town. Is that going to make an impression on anyone? It might be a little underplayed. You know how sometimes you have to hit people over the head with stuff. *(Pause. Smiles.)* But I think it really sings, though. I think it strikes chords in people who really listen. I think a dirty manger has a grace all its own. Shows His way of surprising people by finding power in the small things . . . the ah, commonplace things. It just proves nobody has to be anything special to join in the music. I don't know. I'm not sure people will hear a new song like that, is all I'm saying. *(Looks around. Loudly)* And nobody's going to hear anything if I don't get out of here and to work.

(Pulls notes out of pocket and goes over them. Suddenly G. B. looks at the door U.L.)

Wha . . . what? Did You—? Oh, sorry. Thought I heard You . . . Oh, I know. All in the right time. No, no, I want to do this right, that's for sure. It's an important night. There's no doubt about that.

(He Paces. Stops.)

I just thought of something. I sure hope I'm going out in front of the right people. We need just the right kind of audience for this, I think. We need people who can spread the word. People with some . . . connections. Or who know how to put things together right so other people'll see the pictures. I just hope we're booked in the right place, is all I have to say. This isn't something you can do over again. *(Laughs)* Listen to me, I'm second-guessing everything, as if He didn't know what He was doing. That's my problem. I've got too much time to think in here. I'm starting to let the nerves get to me. OK. *(Takes a breath)* I'm just going to go in and talk to Him. Tell Him that I think the moment is now. Remind Him how much these people need to know what tonight is really all about. *(Heads for the door U.L.)* I'll tell Him people need to hear some good music out there. They've been waiting a long time. I'll tell Him I'm ready to— *(Stops dead. Smiles.)* Oh, hello, Sir. Oh, no, I'm all ready. Yes, I'm sure about it. I've rehearsed a little, too. So, is this it, then? I mean . . . is the word given?

(Pause)

The word is given. *(Claps his hands)* That's wonderful! No, we're all set. That's right. *(Pulls on white jacket. The back reads "The Messengers." Grabs the battered horn case.)* No, the others are ready, too. *(Heads for door D.R.)* Yes, we know the place. Got the address somewhere. *(Pats himself.)* Anyway, we're playing at Bethlehem Fields, right? To the left of the city. Yes, we've got the right music picked out. We're all set. This is going to be great! You arranged this whole thing just perfect, I think. But I got to tell You, it sure isn't the way anybody'd expect it all to happen. No, no! That's the beauty of it, though! *(Looks out)* They're so lucky. You love them very much, don't You? Yeah. I wish they knew it, too. But, what can You do? You've already done it.

(Pause at the door D.R.)

I just thought of something, Sir. I'm sure we're going to scare the daylights out of 'em down there. Give 'em a real shaking. We always seem to do that, don't we. Even when we look like one of them. *(Pulls out piece of paper.)* I'll make a change here, huh? *(Writing)* Right here at the top, I'll add an intro. "Don't be afraid. I'm bringing you good news of great joy!" That should do it.

(G. B. walks through door and out into audience, still reading.)

"Tonight in Bethlehem a Savior has been born to you. He is Christ the Lord! And this will be a sign to you. You will find the baby—" Oh, they're going to love to hear this. It's music to the ears. They've waited a long time to hear a song like this.*

*Start music here

(The lights fade to blackout.)

Director's Tips: Actor energy is key to keeping your audience interested. Be aware of the pacing of the scene. Don't let the actor rush through important lines. Jacket, horn case, chairs, and magazines are really the only props necessary.

Actor's Tips: This is the most important gig he will ever play. Act like it. Conversational speech to yourself, as your thoughts are going external. Maybe you're so excited on the excited points, you stumble over your words. George Costanza is a good model for this. Pick focus points for respective doors. When you're speaking to an imaginary person, see them and react before speaking.

Tips by Chad Schnarr

O Come, All Ye Faithful (AG-1117), words & music by John Francis Wade, arranged by Bruce Greer
   Orchestration, Score and Parts   OR-2531
   Stereo & Split-Trax Accomp CD (both formats included)   MU-5058T
   Acc Cass w/Demo   MU-2531D
"The Word Is Given," **WRAPPINGS** (MC-271), by Lawrence G. Enscoe.

Early Riser

To be performed with the choral octavo *I Will Arise*

Use: Easter

Scripture Reference: John 20:1-4

Theme: Response to the resurrection of Christ.

Cast: MAN—any age
WOMAN—any age

Props: 2 chairs or stools
2 music stands or podiums

Costume Notes: Modern dress

Production Notes:
This piece breaks the reader's theatre format in the final moment.

Running Time: 6-7 minutes

(MAN and WOMAN sitting on chairs or stools. This can be performed in reader's theatre style or as hands-off monologues. If desired, the style of chair can reflect the character. Or the actors can sit in a small mise-en-scène that reflects who they are.)

WOMAN: I'm not an early riser.
I'm not really what they call a morning person.
Once in a while, I'll get up at dawn.
Go outside when the day smells so good and cool, and you get the feeling of possibilities in your stomach, and you think, "Why don't I get up with the sun every morning?"
But you don't.
Most people don't.

But today, I wanted to get up with the sun.

MAN: Saw no reason to get out of bed at all.
The day was going to be like any other day.
That's how it felt to me.
They tell you each day is a new day.
Well, it might be a new day, but it's the same old you, right?

What's the big deal?

I decided I wasn't going to get up.
Pulled the blankets over my eyes.
I decided I was going to sleep in.

WOMAN: I wanted to be the first one there.
 Right in front.
 Before anyone else.

MAN: I wanted to not be there at all.
 I didn't even want to think about it.

WOMAN: Thinking about going excited me.
 Got my heart pumping.
 After all that's happened in my life lately, I needed something to get my
  heart pumping.
 Something to look forward to.

MAN: Thinking about it depressed me.
 Thinking about Him depressed me.
 As far as I was concerned, He died up there on that Cross.
 Nothing changes that.
 Nobody's going to tell me anything different.
 All those people sitting around talking about Him coming back from the
  dead.
 Rising from the *dead?*
 Think about it.
 It depresses me to think about it.
 I'm not going to think about it.
 I'm not going.

WOMAN: I'm going.

 (Pulls on a jacket.)

 I'm going even if nobody else shows up there at all this early.
 At least I could say I went at sunrise.
 I need to start the day that way.
 I need to believe He's alive.
 I have to believe it.

 Even if it is early.
 I'm going.

MAN: I'm not going to be able to sleep.
 Might as well get up.
 Make breakfast.
 Fill a body that needs food and a stomach that doesn't care if it ever eats
  again.

24

(He stands.)

When you're dead, you're dead.
The way it's always been.
The way it should be.
We each get our chance to love, laugh, work, eat, talk, cry, hurt, suffer, die.
Talking about coming back from the dead . . .
Promising people something like that.
It's not natural, is it?
Need to make room for the next ones.

It's not fair.
Making promises you can't keep.

WOMAN: I promised.
I promised myself I would go this morning.
I promised Him.
I keep my promises.

(Starts to leave.)

I promised myself I'd give Him another chance.
That's what He gave me.
Another chance.
He's the only one who's really ever given me that.
Now He seems so far away from me.
Like I never knew Him.

Maybe I'll find Him there.
Maybe I'll find Him again.
Maybe.
Anyway.
I keep my promises.

(She leaves.)

(MAN sits there with his eyes closed, asleep. Suddenly, his eyes pop open.)

MAN: I was falling.
Hate that.
In your sleep, you fall and fall and you don't hit the ground, but you wake up in a panic like you're dying.

(Takes a breath.)

I'm awake now.
No point in trying to get back to sleep now.

(He stands.)

Maybe I'll go later.
More people will probably go later, and I'll blend in more.

Then if nothing happens, I won't feel so alone.
And stupid.

Like I'm feeling now.

Feels like it happens every time.
Put your trust in someone, they let you down.
It's almost a cliché.
I mean, if you really wanted to look at it this way, life really is a whole lot
    of little betrayals. People letting you down.
Events letting you down. Government letting you down. Job letting you
    down.
Dreams letting you down.
God letting you down.
Let down.

Down

He's down in a hole.
The final betrayal.

I'm not going.
Life throws you enough letdowns, no sense in walking wide-eyed into
    one.

I'm not going—

(WOMAN *races in, out of breath.*)

WOMAN: Go.

MAN: I don't want to go.
    Too early.
    I'm not ready.

WOMAN: You should go.

MAN: I'll go later.

WOMAN: I think you should go now.

MAN: Why?

WOMAN: He's there.*

MAN: You mean you felt His presence?

WOMAN: I saw His face.

MAN: His face?

WOMAN: He's there.

MAN: I know He's there. Down in the hole!

WOMAN: Go—

MAN: I don't want to—

WOMAN: He's alive, Peter!

(He stares at her, then grabs his coat and runs out.)

MAN *(as he goes):* John! John! Wake up!

(She stands there. Then she smiles as the lights go to . . .)
*Start music here

(Blackout)

Director's Tips: This is best performed if completely or almost completely memorized. Focus should be out, away from each other, but remaining open the audience. We used music stands for our scripts. The audience needs to see the facial reactions of the two characters. They have to be night and day difference from each other. The actors need to pick up lines quickly in this piece so it doesn't drag too much.

Actor's Tips: Make this piece very conversational. The actors must show how opposite their attitudes towards topic are. Never interact until the very end. It's a quick change for "Peter," so that has to be believable. Hide the secret well. Be genuine and believe your stance on the topic.

Tips by Heather Tinker & Chad Schnarr

I Will Arise (AG-1134), words & music by Chris Machen & Mike Harland, arranged by Richard Kingsmore
  Orchestration, Score and Parts   OR-2554
  Stereo & Split-Trax Accomp CD   MU-5071T
"Early Riser," **SON OF PEW PROMPTER** (MP-774), by Larry and Annie Enscoe.

Other Performance Option:

Perform this piece with *He Is Risen, Hallelujah* (AN-2666). Visit lillenas.com for sound samples.

A Peace of Christ

To be performed with the choral octavo *Table of Grace*

Use: Communion

Theme: Reconciliation

Cast: FRANK—a man in his 30s to 60s
GEORGE—a man in his 30s to 60s

Setting: A church sanctuary

Props: Chairs or pews
4 Communion trays (optional)

Costume Notes: Sunday suits

Production Notes:

This sketch is based on Matthew 5:23-24 and 1 Corinthians 11:23-30, verses about the importance of self-examination and reconciliation when coming to the table of the Lord. Scripture makes it clear that if we come to Communion quarreling and judging others, we will bring judgment down on ourselves.

GEORGE and FRANK are both nursing a long-forgotten grudge. As they serve Communion, they each move from bitterness to accusation, then from remorse to grace and on to personal responsibility and reconciliation.

This sketch can either be performed on a playing area or in the actual aisles of the sanctuary, passing real communion trays through the audience. If you choose the latter option, you will probably need to use radio mikes. Make sure to set up the fact that GEORGE and FRANK are speaking their thoughts and not talking to each other.

The hymn music can either be live or taped. Tape will probably give you more flexibility with the sound.

Running Time: 5 minutes

(The hymn "Jesus Paid It All" is heard in the darkness for a few moments. Lights. A church sanctuary. Chairs face downstage toward the pulpit. FRANK and GEORGE, two ushers, mime passing a Communion tray down the rows. They speak their thoughts, but neither can hear the other.)

"A Peace of Christ" by Lawrence G. and Andrea J. Enscoe is taken from PEW PROMPTER ©
1991 by Lillenas Publishing Company.

FRANK (looking at GEORGE): What's he looking at?

GEORGE (looking at FRANK): What's his problem?

FRANK: I specifically asked not to be put on the serving schedule with GEORGE.

GEORGE: Someone did this on purpose. I was supposed to be serving at 9:30.

(They catch each other's eyes and smile.)

FRANK: There he goes with that Broadway smile. Good Ol' George. Always here for Communion Sunday. Always here for a potluck. But let there be a workday? "Where's George?"

GEORGE: Oh, boy. Frank's got his "holy face" on. Holier than thou's, more like it. What's it been now, Frank? Two, three Sundays you missed. But always here on Communion night. Can't backslide completely, now can we?

FRANK: Know what irritates me about George? Always complaining at church meetings. Sits there and shoots down everybody's ideas like clay pigeons.

GEORGE: Know what really gets my goat? Frank's negative attitude. Forever griping about what needs to get done, then sitting on his duff.

FRANK: You know, it's people like George that make me dread coming to worship.

GEORGE: You know, it's people like Frank that keep folks away from churches.

(They have finished passing out the Communion bread. They take trays to the pulpit and hand them to the "minister." The organ stops playing. FRANK and GEORGE take a Communion bread.)

FRANK/GEORGE: Sure glad I'm not a hypocrite. Like him.

(They look at each other.)

"Do this in remembrance of me."

(They put the bread in their mouths. The organ starts playing "Nothing but the Blood." FRANK and GEORGE take the "trays" of cups.)

FRANK: What happened to you, George?

GEORGE (same time): What happened to you, Frank?

(They start passing "trays" down the rows.)

GEORGE: I remember when I used to look up to you. You seemed like you had it all together. Now my stomach twists into a knot every time I see you.

FRANK: One of the reasons Ellie and I stayed here so long was because of you and Elaine. You were so friendly. Cared about us from the beginning. Now I can get irritated just looking at you.

FRANK/GEORGE: When did that start happening?

(They catch each other's eyes. Sad smiles.)

GEORGE: Boy, did I just have a memory. Remember when we planned that "Italian Night" fund-raiser? Nobody came, and we all ate spaghetti for lunch for about six months!

FRANK: You know, I can still remember fishing over July Fourth weekend. Waking up and doing devotions at sunrise. Eating tuna sandwiches because we didn't catch anything but ticks.

GEORGE: You came over and checked on me every day for two weeks while I was in the worst of my pneumonia.

FRANK: All those "anonymous" checks in my mailbox when I was out of work.

GEORGE: Now we only see each other at church events. Even then we avoid each other.

FRANK: Make sure we're not in the same discussion groups.

FRANK/GEORGE: What did you do to hurt me?

FRANK: I really don't remember exactly what it was. Maybe it was a lot of things put together.

GEORGE: Maybe it was nothing.

(They glance at each other.)

FRANK: Was it my fault? Did I expect too much out of you?

GEORGE: Was it me? Did I put you up on a pedestal?

(They walk up the aisle toward the "minister.")

FRANK: I wonder if he remembers what we're really fighting about?

GEORGE: *I wonder if he knows why we're so mad at each other?
*Start music here

(They hand up the "trays" and take a cup for themselves.)

FRANK/GEORGE: Maybe I should ask him.

(They face each other with the cups.)
    The peace of Christ.

(They freeze with hands up, holding the cups. The lights fade to:

(Blackout.)

Director's Tips: Timing is a must on this piece. All elements must be rehearsed with prior to performance. If extras are used, they must attend rehearsal. Consult the pastor as to whether actual sacraments should be used, or if they should be pantomimed. You can set 12-15 people up in 3 rows *(4 or 5* *in each)* on stage, or set the chairs *(no people)* and pantomime passing a plate.

The audience needs to see the emotions played out through the actors' actions, so encourage ways each actor can express those emotions through the stage business without losing control. Controlled physicality will get a better reaction than extreme actions given the content of the scene.

Actor's Tips: Since the dialogue is nothing more than internal thoughts, don't be tempted to fully internalize the characterization as well. Avoid any possibility of it looking like you're talking to each other. The crowning moment of this piece is at the end. Give it it's due, and set it up.

For the eating of the bread, avoid eye contact and any sentimentality of the act. For the cup, pause, look at each other. The words "Peace of Christ" are said with the realization that is what was missing from their relationship and that "Peace" is revered. Control emotions, keep it simple.

Tips by Chad Schnarr & Chris Todd

Table of Grace (AG-1087), words & music by Connie Harrington & Anna Hutto; arranged by Marty Parks
   Orchestration, Score and Parts   OR-2469
   Stereo & Split-Trax Accomp CD (both formats included)   MU-5045T
   Acc Cass W/Demo   MU-2469D
"A Peace of Christ," **PEW PROMPTER** (MP-662), by Lawrence G. and Andrea J. Enscoe

The Stone

To be performed with the choral octavo *Reach the World*

Use: Missions/Great Commission

Theme: "The Stone" deals specifically with the forgiveness and conversion of Mary Magdalene, but in a broader sense it talks about forgiveness of all sinners and our obligation to share what the Lord has done for us with others who so desperately need Him.

Cast: MARY MAGDALENE

Costume Notes: A costume in keeping with the piece can be used, but current fashion may help the audience "put themselves in her place."

Production Notes: This piece works best with very little set or props. The vision of what Mary is saying must be created in the mind of the observer.

Running Time: 5 minutes

MARY: They were days of endless peril, all of us afraid of our own shadows. We rarely did more than whisper of the days' events, for fear of whose ears might be listening, trying to catch us and carry us away.

I am ashamed to admit that my terror had so overwhelmed me that I actually considered foregoing the trip to the garden with the others. Believe me, I had been sneered at by the mighty Roman guards before, but since they had taken our Lord to His death, things had been different. A Jew, let alone a Jewish woman, who was also a known believer, was a prize. Many times I washed at the river, only to see others beaten and dragged away to a fate that I can scarcely imagine.

When Jesus was alive it was different. The Roman pigs were afraid of Him. They didn't admit it, but you could see the apprehension in their eyes whenever He came around. They trembled behind their mighty swords when He did nothing more than look their way. After He was gone, they decided to take revenge on His followers, and especially the women. A simple walk to the market became a risk of one's life. And so, many of us, myself included, locked our doors and kept our lamps on a low light, whispering prayers far into the night, hoping that the footsteps outside would pass on down the street, leaving us one more hour of safety.

I made a point of walking with my face down, speaking to no one, hoping to complete my business if possible, without incident. Whenever I heard voices approaching I hurried to a doorway, hoping to fade into the background of the dusty street. On the morning of that third day I awoke in a cold sweat, the air was filled with a current of excitement and anxiety. He had spoken to us of this day, many times, but I was in the dark about our future. We were followers of the Son of God, yet too afraid to step out into the light of day. As I prepared my basket of spices I could feel His presence with me, and I wanted to throw my windows open and shout His name into the morning air, but the pounding of my heart rang louder with each breath I took and I finally resolved that today I would stay in. The Lord knew that I loved Him. He would not want me to put myself in danger.

I sat on the bench near the fire and tried to warm the ice away from my aching soul, sorry for myself, sorry for the people who would never know. Then suddenly the room faded before me and I was standing in the streets of the city. The sun was hot on my face, and I could taste the dust in my mouth. My garment was torn and my hair disheveled, and all around me stood an angry, hungry mob. Their eyes burned with the passion of the kill, and in their hands they held my death sentence.

My fear so excited them, they stood for just a moment enjoying their power over me, savoring its intoxicating strength, before they would at last destroy their prey beneath an onslaught of shouts and stones. They were so completely spellbound that they didn't even notice the man pushing His way through the crowd and into the center of the bloodthirsty circle. I saw Him just as He emerged from behind the chief priest, and at the moment of His appearing, my fear dispelled into the mist of His peace. He walked to me as though the others had vanished, their stones turned to dust, their hatred diffused. They shouted to Him to come away from the woman and leave her to her fate or surely He would die with her. Did He even hear them? I couldn't tell. He only bent to help me up from the jaw of my grave and said that I was forgiven. Then He sent me on my way without need for explanation or pleading. As I began to run from the crowd, my shame and hatred dropped behind me at the feet of those who sought to kill me. I looked back only once as I ran, but in that instant my heart was bound to His in an unbreakable force. I knew that forever I would belong to Him.

The room cleared, and I was on my face before the fire, weeping over the scene that had just played, aghast at my own lack of courage. Could I deny the one who had pulled me from the darkness of my own sin, the one who risked everything to stand by my side in the midst of savage violence? Could I hide in my fear while others desperately stood on the dusty streets of the city, waiting for the Savior to lift them out of their open graves. *Even now, their frightened souls called to me to bring Him to them. I pushed the door open and let the light flood my heart. I am coming, Lord, I could hear myself whispering. I am coming.

*Start music here

34

Director's Tips: Talk through the piece and discuss the emotional highs and lows represented in the script with your actor. Help shape specific focal points, and get inside the parts of the piece where it is most natural to have the actor gesture and move within the acting space.

Actor's Tips: Tempo and being able to tell the story well are important. Deliberately work on how each part of the script is delivered—when the lines pick up in pace; when to slow down. The intensity of the piece must be built gradually and naturally. In your mind's eye, picture the events you are describing to help communicate those thoughts to the audience.

Reach the World (AN-1868), words & music by Mark Bishop, arranged by
  Richard Kingsmore
  Orchestration, Score and Parts   OR-2416
  Stereo Accomp CD   MU-5507T
  Acc Cass W/Demo   MU-2416D
"The Stone," **WORSHIP DRAMA LIBRARY, VOL. 3** (MP-712), by Kristin Witt.

Other Performance Option:

Perform this piece with *Go Light Your World* (AG-1034). Visit lillenas.com for sound samples.

Song Information

I Need You More with *I Need Thee Every Hour*   AN-8113
Words & Music by Lindell Cooley & Bruce Hayes
Arranged by Marty Parks
Listening Cassette   TA-610C
Listening CD   DC-610
Orchestration, Score and Parts   OR-2515
Stereo & Split-Trax Accomp CD (Both Formats Included)   MU-5533T
Acc Cass W/Demo   MU-2515D

You Are God   AG-1099
Words & Music by Sam, Jesse, Joe, John, & James Katina
Arranged by Richard Kingsmore
Octavo Demo Cassette   TA-607C
Octavo Demo CD   DC-607
Orchestration, Score and Parts   OR-2490
Stereo & Split-Trax Accomp CD (Both Formats Included)   MU-5049T
Acc Cass W/Demo   MU-2490D

A Cradle in the Shadow of the Cross   AN-3927
Words & Music by Dorothy L. Smith
Arranged by Richard Kingsmore
Orchestration, Score and Parts   OR-2455
Stereo & Split-Trax Accomp CD (Both Formats Included)   MU-5519T
Acc Cass W/Demo   MU-2455D

O Come All Ye Faithful   AG-1117
Words & Music by John Francis Wade
Arranged by Bruce Greer
Orchestration, Score and Parts   OR-2531
Stereo & Split-Trax Accomp CD (Both Formats Included)   MU-5058T
Acc Cass W/Demo MU-2531D

I Will Arise   AG-1134
Words & Music by Chris Machen & Mike Harland
Arranged by Richard Kingsmore
Orchestration, Score and Parts   OR-2554
Stereo & Split-Trax Accomp CD   MU-5071T

Table of Grace   AG-1087
Words & Music by Connie Harrington & Anna Hutto
Arranged by Marty Parks
Orchestration, Score and Parts   OR-2469
Stereo & Split-Trax Accomp CD (Both Formats Included)   MU-5045T
Acc Cass W/Demo   MU-2469D

Reach the World   AN-1868
Words & Music by Mark Bishop
Arranged by Richard Kingsmore
Orchestration, Score and Parts   OR-2416
Stereo Accomp CD   MU-5507T
Acc Cass W/Demo   MU-2416D

Also available—a video resource with all 7 sketches! MU-796V.